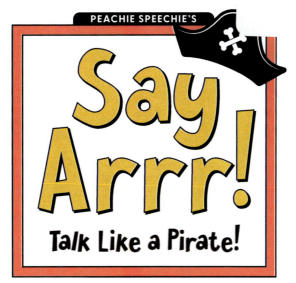

Copyright ©2022 by Meredith Avren

Written by Meredith Avren, M.Ed., CCC-SLP
Illustrated by Josh Avren

All rights reserved. No part of this book, may be reproduced, transmitted, or stored in an information retrieval system in any form or by any means, graphic, electronic, or mechanical, including photocopying, taping and recording, without prior written permission from the publisher. In accordance of the U.S. Copyright Act of 1976, any violation is unlawful piracy and theft of the author's and illustrator's intellectual property.

If you would like to use material from this book other than for personal use, prior written premission must be obtained by contacting the publisher at permissions@avrenbooks.com. Thank you for your support of the creators' rights.

Say Arrr: Talk Like A Pirate - First Edition 2023

Library of Congress Catalog Card Number Pending

978-0-9995964-5-6
10 9 8 7 6 5 4 3 2 1

Published by Avren Books™

PEACHIE SPEECHIE'S
Additional Resources

Speech Sound Handbook

R Sound Chaining

I Can Say the R Sound

Coarticulation for the R Sound

Thank you for supporting our small business!

—Meredith & Josh

ALL RIGHTS RESERVED ©PEACHIESPEECHIE.COM

Talk Like a Pirate: Say Arrr!

Table of Contents

6	Talk Like a Pirate Vocabulary
7	Anatomy Instruction
8	Two Ways to Say *Arrr*
9	Video Worksheet
10-17	Retroflex *Arrr* Step-by-Step
18	Retroflex *Arrr* Pirate Map
19-26	Bunched *Arrr* Step-by-Step
27	Bunched *Arrr* Pirate Map
28-31	*Arrr* Practice in Isolation
32-33	Minimal Pairs
34-39	Sound-by-Sound® Activities
40-43	Word-Level Practice
44-45	Word Search & Answer Key
46	Coarticulation for *Arrr*
47	Phrase-Level Practice
48-53	Sentence-Level Practice
54	Chaining for the R Sound
55-56	Pirate Story & Comprehension Questions
57-61	Pirate Hat Craft
63-69	Shark Bite Game
71-81	Peachie Speechie Giant Mouth Visuals
83	About the Author

Information for the Speech-Language Pathologist

Thank you for using this workbook, Say *Arrr*: Talk Like a Pirate, with your students! I hope you find it engaging and helpful.

When using these materials with your students, you'll want to have a few items on hand.

- A mirror, so the student can watch their mouth movements as they practice.
- Tongue depressor or lollipop, to point out and increase awareness of articulators.
- Scissors, crayons/markers, or dot markers and tape to complete the craft portions of this workbook.

A few additional tips:
- If the child is having difficulty differentiating tongue and jaw movements, you may want to try using a bite block. Place the bite block between the child's molars on one side to stabilize their jaw as they practice moving their tongue independently of the jaw. They can look in the mirror and practice lateral bracing and/or curling their tongue tip up and back with the bite block in place. Once they have success in isolating tongue movement, practice saying *Arrr* without the bite block.
- Lip rounding is sometimes present during production of R, but it is not a key articulatory requirement. Therefore, I rarely prompt my students to push out/round their lips. However, if your student is producing a close approximation of *Arrr*, you may want to instruct them to push their lips out a little bit, into more of a square shape (not totally rounded) to see if that helps.
- Through my clinical experience, I've found it helpful to practice slowly at first, focusing on the individual steps. Immediately after my students were stimulable using the steps, I transitioned to more natural sounding word level practice.

More R Sound Materials
The R sound is my favorite thing to work on in speech therapy sessions. With over a decade of experience treating students with R sound errors, I've created a bunch of materials and videos dedicated to this sound. **Scan the QR codes below** and take your R sound therapy to the next level!

I Can Say the R Sound

Coarticulation for the R Sound

R Sound Chaining

Free Video Library

Today we are going to talk like pirates!

The R Sound can be a tricky one to teach and to learn. This workbook is designed to make the R sound fun with step-by-step instructions to get your students sounding like pirates and practicing their best *Arrrrr!*

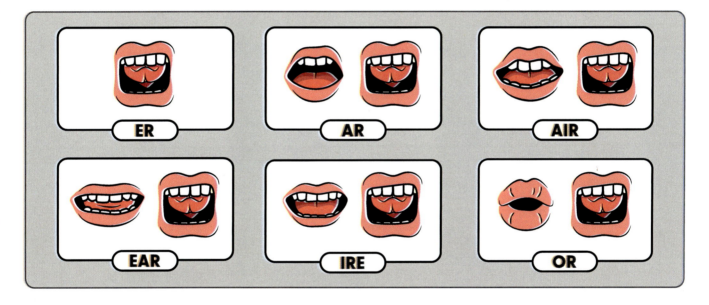

The R sound can be more challenging in certain contexts for different individuals. In this workbook, we will focus on *Arrr*. Why?

- The /a/ sound facilitates tongue root retraction, creating the pharyngeal constriction necessary for an accurate R sound.
- The Arrr context can be easily taught with either bunched or retroflex tongue positions and can be produced with the jaw slightly more open for increased visibility of the tongue in a mirror.
- It's fun! You can call it the Pirate Sound and get students happily engaged in the lesson through exciting pirate-themed activities.

Please note that in this workbook, when AR or *Arrr* is written, it refers to /ɑɹ/ as in the word "car". When *Ahh* is written, it refers to the /ɑ/ vowel, as in "pond". This workbook was designed to be child and parent-friendly, so International Phonetic Alphabet (IPA) symbols are not used on the instructional or activity pages.

International Talk Like a Pirate Day

September 19th is International Talk Like a Pirate Day, a silly holiday created in 1995 by two friends in Oregon, John Baurs and Mark Summers. They came up with the idea while playing racquetball and saying "Arrgh!" whenever they got hurt. They decided to spend a whole day each year talking like pirates, greeting their friends with "Ahoy matey!" instead of "Hello!"

The holiday gained popularity when a writer published an article about it in the Miami Herald, and now it is celebrated each year by many people. You can join in the fun! Learn some pirate vocabulary words and be ready for the next September 19th.

Pirate Vocabulary

Accord = Agreement
Ahoy = Hello
Arrr = Expresses frustration or excitement
Avast = Stop
Aye = Yes
Booty = Treasure
Buccaneer = Pirate
Cutlass = Sword
Doubloons = Coins or money
Hearties = Friends
Jolly roger = The pirate flag
Landlubber = Someone who doesn't know much about the sea
Lass = Lady
Lad = Young man
Marooned = Stranded on an island
Matey = Friend
Plunder = To steal
Sea shanty = A song pirates sing
Shiver me timbers = An expression of surprise

Talk Like a Pirate: Prerequisite Knowledge

Learn yer anatomy, matey!

Before you dive into the *Arrr* sound, you need to get familiar with the parts of your mouth and tongue. Look at the diagram below, and color it with crayons or markers. Talk about the different parts of the tongue with your speech-language pathologist. Then, look in the mirror and identify the different parts in your own mouth.

With the help of your SLP, use a tongue depressor, straw, or lollipop to touch the different parts of your tongue as you look in the mirror. You can also touch the "tongue bracing spots" or "anchor points" just inside your back teeth.

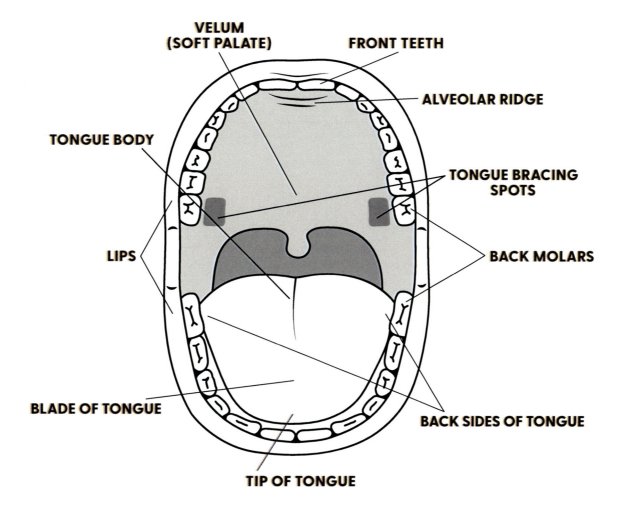

Two ways to say Arrr: Bunched & Retroflex

There are two main tongue positions for the R sound: bunched and retroflex. When saying *Arrr* like a pirate, you will start with the *Ahh* sound and then move your tongue into place for either the bunched or the retroflex R. Use the visuals below as you discuss each tongue position with your speech therapist. You can try both positions and see which results in a better *Arrr* sound.

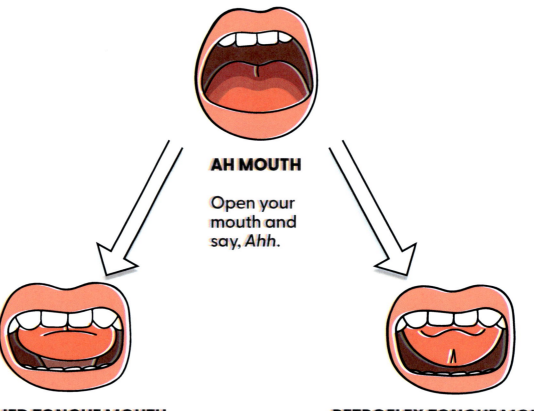

AH MOUTH

Open your mouth and say, *Ahh*.

BUNCHED TONGUE MOUTH

Lift the back sides of your tongue up to touch the insides of your back teeth. Close your jaw a little bit.

RETROFLEX TONGUE MOUTH

Lift your tongue tip up and curl it back. Close your jaw a little bit.

Scan to view Bunched R Video

Scan to view Retroflex R Video

© PEACHIESPEECHIE.COM
Mouths and other visuals may not be transmitted, copied, duplicated or reproduced in whole or part by any means.

Talk Like a Pirate Video

VIEW THIS VIDEO AT PEACHIESPEECHIE.COM/VIDEOS

Scan the QR code or visit PeachieSpeechie.com/videos to access the free video titled Talk Like a Pirate: Say *Arrr*. Follow along with speech-language pathologist Meredith Avren as she guides you through the movements to say a clear *Arrr* sound.

Steps to Retroflex Arrr

Say, *Ahh*.

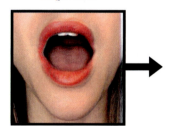

Curl your tongue tip up and back.

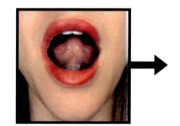

Close your jaw a little bit.

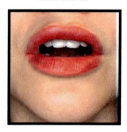

Steps to Bunched Arrr

Say, *Ahh*.

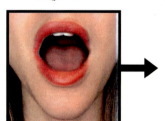

Life the back sides of your tongue up to the insides of your back teeth.

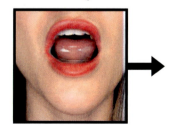

Close your jaw a little bit.

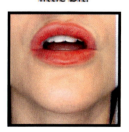

Practice saying *Arrr* like a pirate using the video and visuals above. Each time you practice, check one of the boxes.

◯◯◯◯◯◯◯◯◯
◯◯◯◯◯◯◯◯◯

© PEACHIESPEECHIE.COM
Mouths and other visuals may not be transmitted, copied, duplicated or reproduced in whole or part by any means.

Talk Like a Pirate: Step 1

Voice on, me hearties!

The first step to saying *Arrr* is to turn your voice on and say, *Ahh*. Look in the mirror and open your mouth. Say, *Ahh*.

Retroflex R

Talk Like a Pirate: Step 2

The 2nd step to saying *Arrr* is to **lift the tongue tip and curl it back**.

The back sides of your tongue will lift too, touching just inside your back teeth. Remember, your voice will be on. Look in the mirror as you practice.

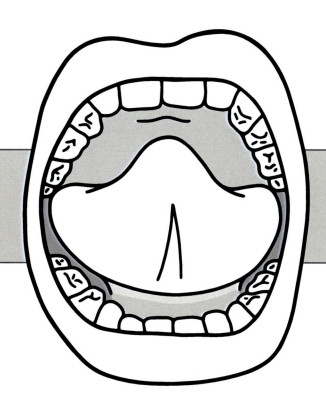

As you say, *Ahh*, lift the tongue tip and curl it back.

Talk Like a Pirate: Step 3

The 3rd step to saying *Arrr* is **closing your jaw a little bit**.

With your voice on and your tongue tip curled back, close your jaw a little bit.

You will hear the sound change from *Ahh* to *Arrr*. Way to go, matey!

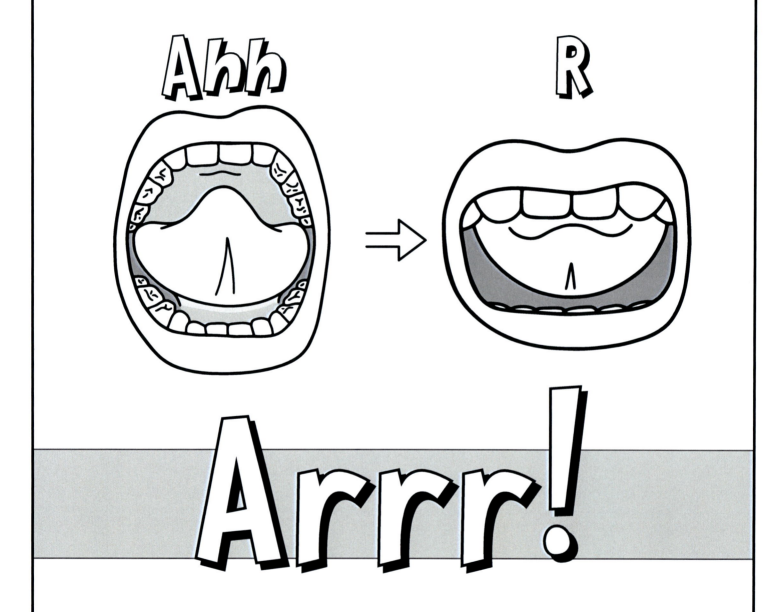

Talk Like a Pirate: Say Arrr!

Retroflex R

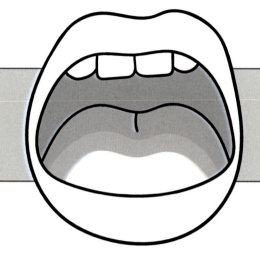

Say, Ahh.

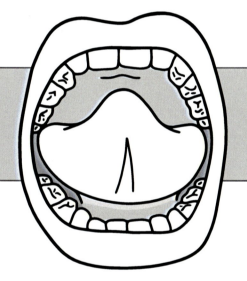

Lift your tongue tip and curl it back.

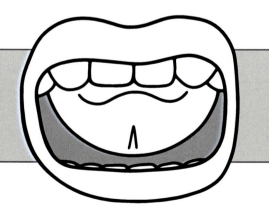

Close your jaw a little bit. Listen as the sound changes from *Ahh* to *Arrr*.

Peachie Speechie's Photo Visuals for Arrr!

Look at the photo visuals below. Follow the steps and practice saying *Arrr* like a pirate. Tip: Use a mirror to look at your own mouth. Try to make your mouth look like the mouth in the photos.

Retroflex R

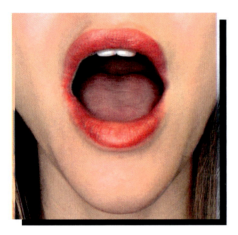

Say, *Ahh*.

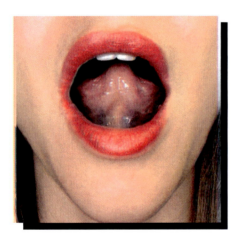

Lift your tongue tip and curl it back.

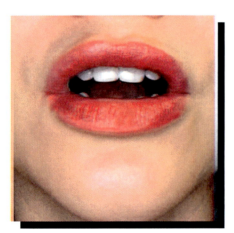

Close your jaw a little bit. Listen as the sound changes from *Ahh* to *Arrr*.

Pirate Practice: Say Arrr

Retroflex R

Directions: Look at the step by step photos below. Follow the steps to say *Arrr* like a pirate. Each time you say it, mark one of the circles. If desired, you can mark a ✓ for accurate productions, a ~ for close approximations, and ✗ for incorrect productions.

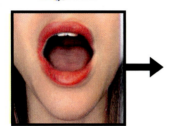

Say, Ahh.

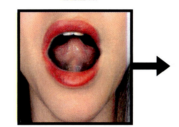

Curl your tongue tip up and back.

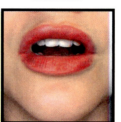

Close your jaw a little bit.

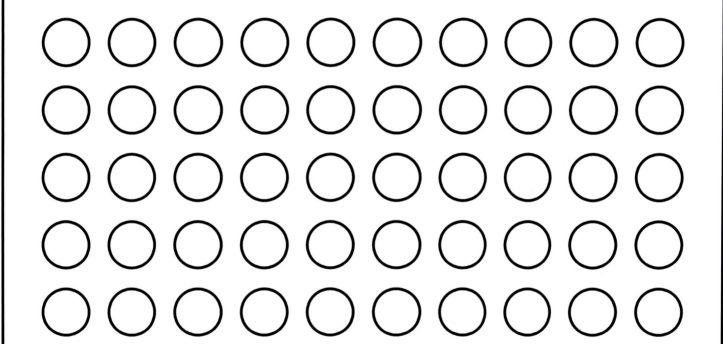

Self rating: How did I sound?

Talk Like a Pirate

Now that you've practiced saying *Arrr* with the step-by-step directions, it's time to practice saying it faster and faster. This can help prepare you for saying the *Arrr* sound in words and conversational speech.

Start by saying it slowly. Say, *Ahh*, and then gradually move your tongue into place for the R sound, so it sounds like *Arrr*.

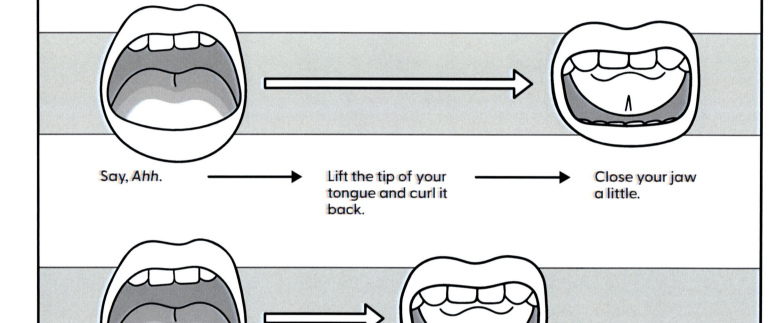

Say, *Ahh*. → Lift the tip of your tongue and curl it back. → Close your jaw a little.

Next, say it quicker. Start by saying *Ahh* and quickly moving your tongue into place for the R sound.

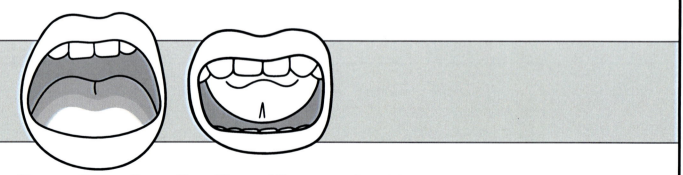

Now, say it even faster. You will sound like a true pirate! *Arrr!*

Trace and Say Arrr: Retroflex

Directions: Start by saying, *Ahh*, as indicated on the left of the page. Then, trace your finger or a crayon across the dotted line as you lift your tongue to say a clear pirate *Arrr* sound. For additional practice, trace each line multiple times, using different color crayons.

Arrr you ready, matey?!

It's time to practice your best pirate *Arrr* sound! Use a crayon or marker to trace along the treasure map as you say your sounds. Say, *Ahh* as you trace along the dotted lines. Then, move your tongue into place for *Arrr* when you reach the dots. When you reach the X on the map you're done! For an extra challenge, you can complete the map multiple times, using a different color marker each time.

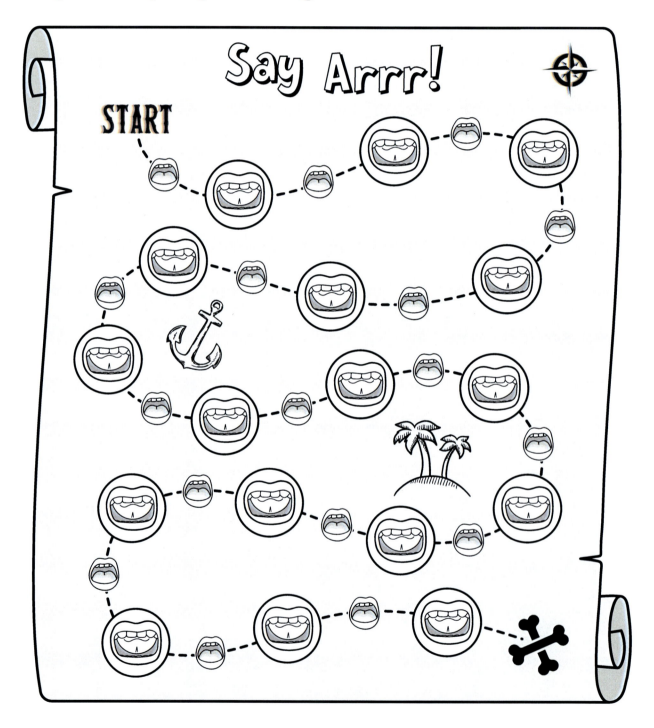

Talk Like a Pirate: Step 1

Turn your voice on, matey!

The first step to saying *Arrr* is to turn your voice on and say, *Ahh*. Look in the mirror and open your mouth. Say, *Ahh*.

Bunched R

Bunched R

Talk Like a Pirate: Step 2

The second step to saying *Arrr* is **anchoring the tongue**. When a pirate drops the anchor, the boat stays in place. It doesn't float away. Similarly, when we anchor the tongue, we keep it in place.

The back sides of the tongue need to lift up to the insides of the back teeth. You can call these the **anchor points** or tongue bracing spots. The back sides are going to stay anchored there. Don't drop them! Look in the mirror as you practice.

Tip: Make the back of the tongue wide as you press the back sides of the tongue into the insides of the back teeth. You'll feel **tension** in your tongue as you do this.

- Lift the back sides of the tongue up & anchor them inside the back teeth.
- Hold your tongue in this position.

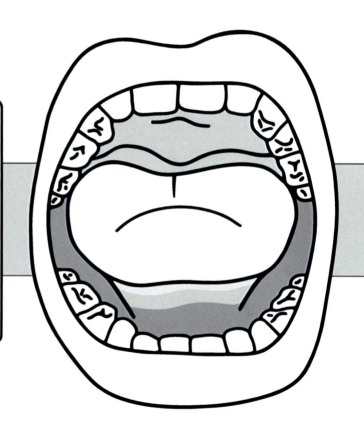

Talk Like a Pirate: Step 3

The third step to saying *Arrr* is **lifting the front of the tongue and closing the jaw**.

With your voice on and the back sides of your tongue anchored to the insides of the back teeth, lift the tongue tip/blade just a little bit, and close your jaw.

You will hear the sound go from *Ahh* to *Arrr*. Now you sound like a pirate! Way to go, matey!

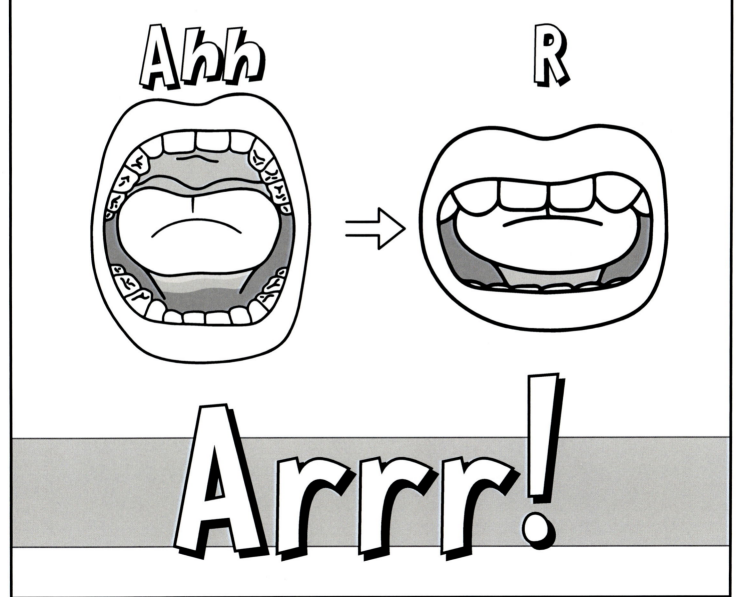

Talk Like a Pirate: Say Arrr!

Bunched R

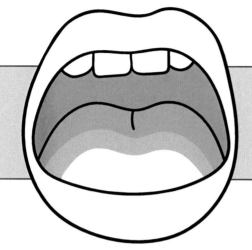

Say, *Ahh*.

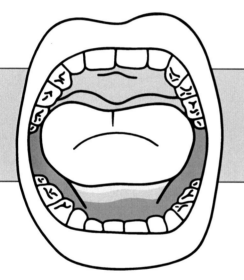

Lift the back sides up to the insides of your back teeth.

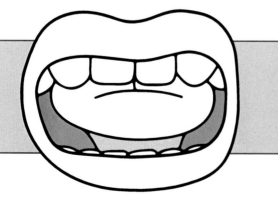

Lift the front of your tongue a little bit and close your jaw. Listen as the sound changes from *Ahh* to *Arrr*.

Peachie Speechie's Photo Visuals for Arrr!

Bunched R

Look at the photo visuals below. Follow the steps and practice saying *Arrr* like a pirate. Tip: Use a mirror to look at your own mouth. Try to make your mouth look like the mouth in the photos.

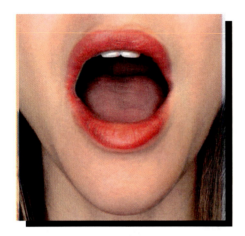

Say, *Ahh*.

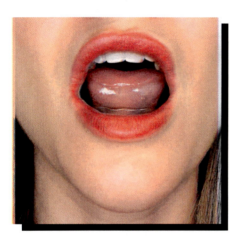

Lift the back sides of your tongue up to the insides of your back teeth.

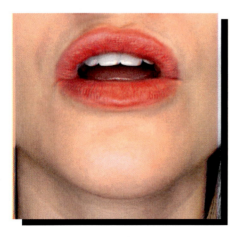

Lift the front of your tongue a little bit and close your jaw. Listen as the sound changes from *Ahh* to *Arrr*.

Bunched R

Pirate Practice: Say Arrr

Directions: Look at the step by step photos below. Follow the steps to say *Arrr* like a pirate. Each time you say it, mark one of the circles. If desired, you can mark a ✓ for accurate productions, a ~ for close approximations, and ✗ for incorrect productions.

Say, *Ahh*.

Life the back sides of your tongue up to the insides of your back teeth.

Close your jaw a little bit.

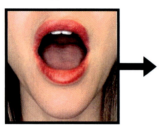
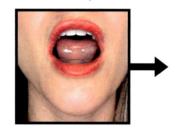
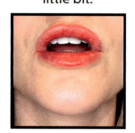

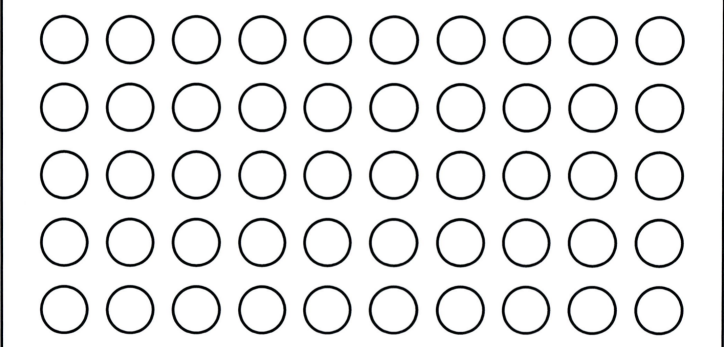

Self rating: How did I sound?

Talk Like a Pirate

Now that you've practiced saying *Arrr* with the step-by-step directions, it's time to practice saying it faster and faster. This can help prepare you for saying the *Arrr* sound in words and conversational speech.

Start by saying it slowly. Say, *Ahh*, and then gradually move your tongue into place for the R sound, so it sounds like *Arrr*.

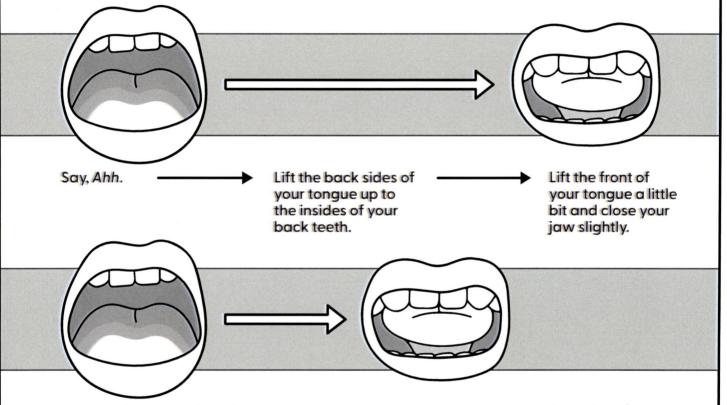

Say, *Ahh*. → Lift the back sides of your tongue up to the insides of your back teeth. → Lift the front of your tongue a little bit and close your jaw slightly.

Next, say it quicker. Start by saying *Ahh* and quickly moving your tongue into place for the R sound.

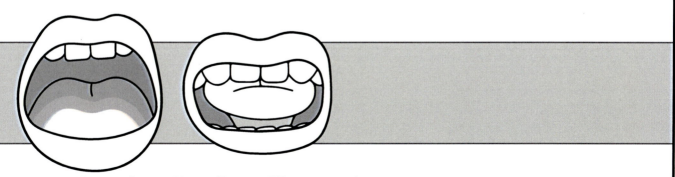

Now, say it even faster. You will sound like a true pirate! *Arrr!*

Trace and Say Arrr: Bunched

Directions: Start by saying, *Ahh*, as indicated on the left of the page. Then, trace your finger or a crayon across the dotted line as you lift your tongue to say a clear pirate *Arrr* sound. For additional practice, trace each line multiple times, using different color crayons.

Arrr you ready, matey?!

It's time to practice your best pirate *Arrr* sound! Use a crayon or marker to trace along the treasure map as you say your sounds. Say, *Ahh* as you trace along the dotted lines. Then, move your tongue into place for *Arrr* when you reach the dots. When you reach the X on the map you're done! For an extra challenge, you can complete the map multiple times, using a different color marker each time.

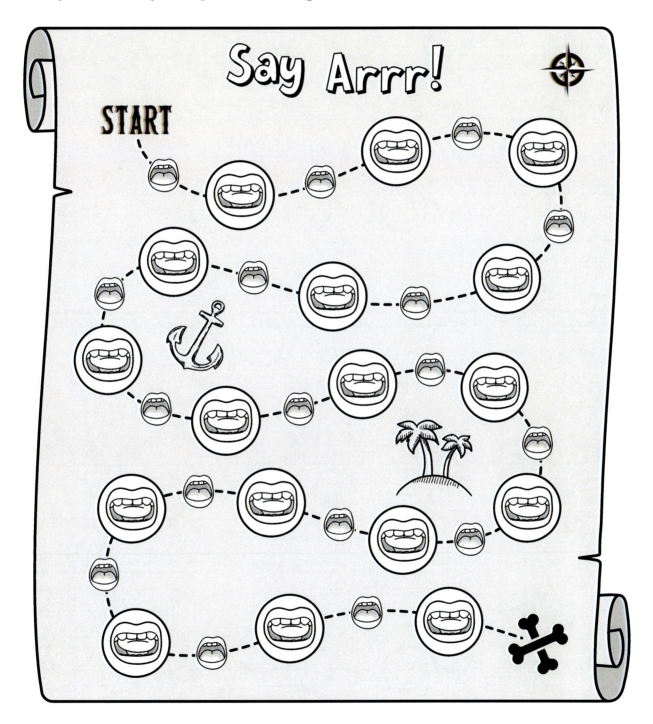

Talk Like a Pirate: Say Arrr!

The characters below are saying, Arrr! You are going to say it, too! Each time you practice saying Arrr, check one of the dots. When you're done, you will have practiced 50 times. Way to go, matey!

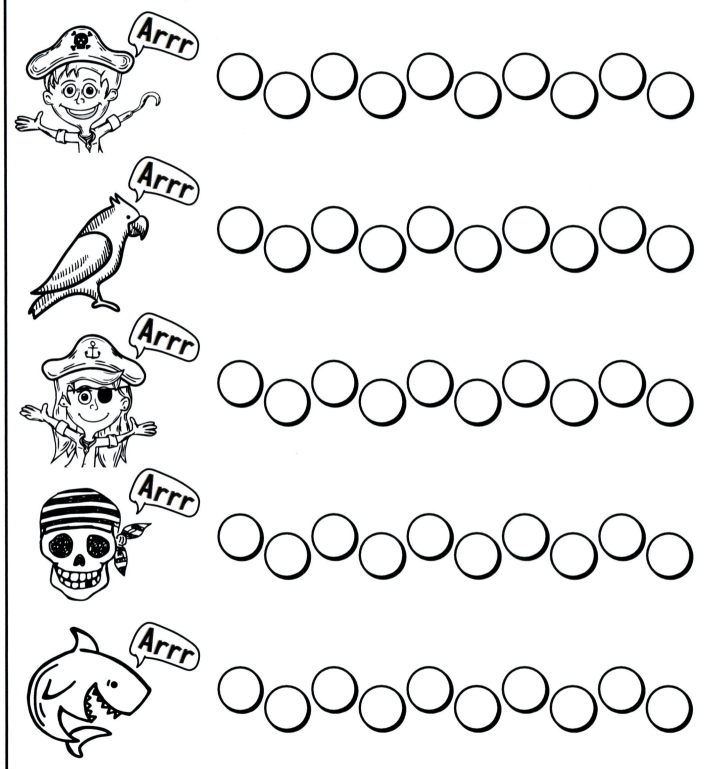

Say Arrr 100 Times

Directions: *Arrr* you ready for a challenge, matey? Say, *Arrr* like a pirate 100 times. Each time, check one of the coins below.

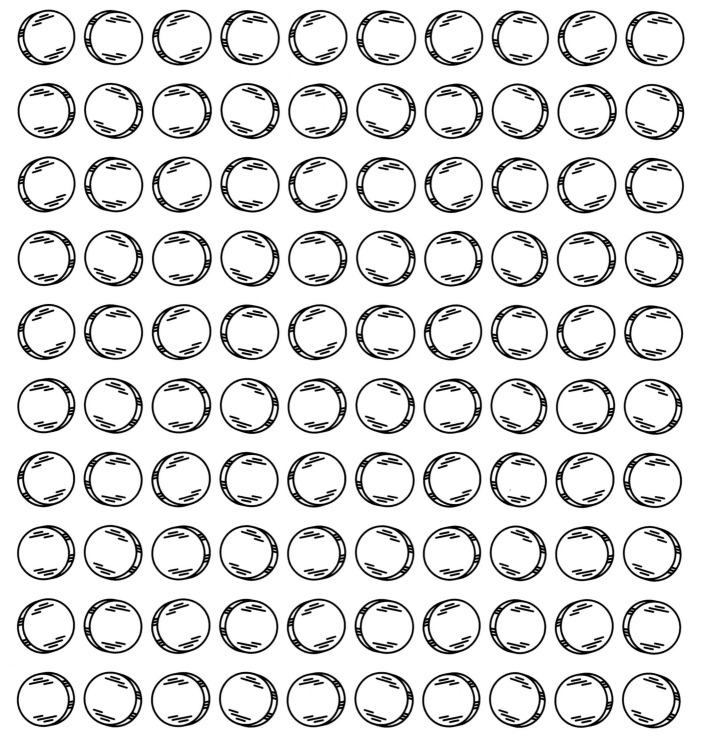

Roll and Race Arrr

Directions: Roll a die and mark a corresponding icon on the page. Each time you do this, practice saying your best pirate *Arrr* sound. Then, rate your performance using the rating scale at the bottom of the page. If playing with a partner, the first person to complete a row wins. If playing independently, see how many rows you can complete during one speech therapy session.

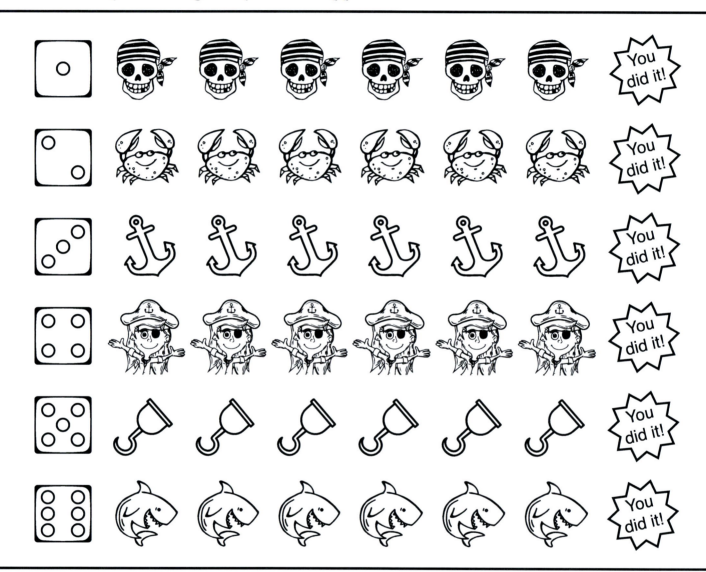

Self rating: How did I sound?

Talk Like a Pirate: Spin and Practice

Directions: Use a paperclip and a pencil to make a spinner as shown. Spin the paperclip and practice the *Arrr* word it lands on. Then, color in one picture below. Repeat this until all of the pictures are colored in.

Pirate Pairs: Minimal Pairs for Arrr

If you leave the *Arrr* sound out of a word, it can change the meaning of the word completely. Without the *Arrr* sound, "jar" becomes "jaw", for example. Practice saying each of the words below. First, say it without *Arrr*. Next, put your tongue up and say it with a clear pirate *Arrr* sound.

Caw

Car

Jaw

Jar

Baa

Bar

Ahh

Arrr

© PEACHIESPEECHIE.COM
Mouths and other visuals may not be transmitted, copied, duplicated or reproduced in whole or part by any means.

Pirate Pairs: Minimal Pairs for Arrr

If you leave the *Arrr* sound out of a word, it can change the meaning of the word completely. Without the *Arrr* sound, "jar" becomes "jaw", for example. Practice saying each of the words below. First, say it without *Arrr*. Next, put your tongue up and say it with a clear pirate *Arrr* sound.

Shock

Shark

Cod

Card

Hot

Heart

Dot

Dart

Arrr Words: Sound-By-Sound®

Retroflex R

Start by saying the *Ahh* sound. Then, move your tongue into place for the *Arrr* sound (like a pirate!). Then, add the last sound. Finally, say it together quickly to make the word.

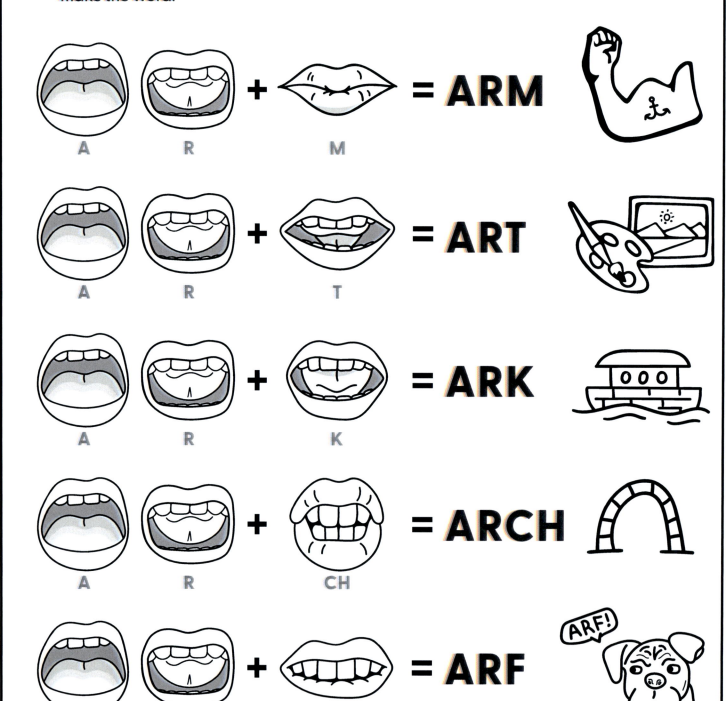

Bunched R

Arrr Words: Sound-By-Sound®

Start by saying the *Ahh* sound. Then, move your tongue into place for the *Arrr* sound (like a pirate!). Then, add the last sound. Finally, say it together quickly to make the word.

  +  = **ARM**
A   R   M

  +  = **ART**
A   R   T

  +  = **ARK**
A   R   K

 +  = **ARCH**
A   R   CH

 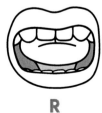 +  = **ARF**
A   R   F

© PEACHIESPEECHIE.COM
Mouths and other visuals may not be transmitted, copied, duplicated or reproduced in whole or part by any means.

Sound-by-Sound® Arrr Practice: Word Builder Web

Retroflex R

Directions: Start with the sounds at the top of the page. Then, move your mouth to add *Arrr* to the end of the word. Say it slowly at first, and then say it faster. Bonus: Can you make a sentence with the word?

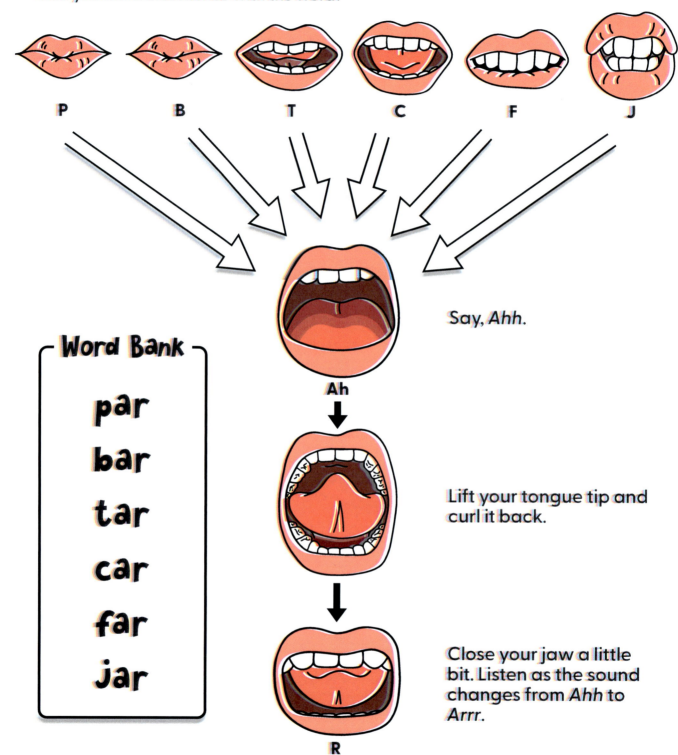

P   B   T   C   F   J

Say, *Ahh*.

Ah

Lift your tongue tip and curl it back.

Close your jaw a little bit. Listen as the sound changes from *Ahh* to *Arrr*.

R

Word Bank

par
bar
tar
car
far
jar

Retroflex R

Sound-by-Sound® Arrr Practice

Directions: Say each word below. Say it slowly at first, and then say it faster. Mark a box each time you say it. BONUS: Can you make a sentence with the word?

P A R	☐ ☐ ☐ ☐ ☐
B A R	☐ ☐ ☐ ☐ ☐
T A R	☐ ☐ ☐ ☐ ☐
C A R	☐ ☐ ☐ ☐ ☐
F A R	☐ ☐ ☐ ☐ ☐
J A R	☐ ☐ ☐ ☐ ☐

© peachiespeechie.com
Mouths and other visuals may not be transmitted, copied, duplicated or reproduced in whole or part by any means.

Sound-by-Sound® Arrr Practice: Word Builder Web

Bunched R

Directions: Start with the sounds at the top of the page. Then, move your mouth to add *Arrr* to the end of the word. Say it slowly at first, and then say it faster. Bonus: Can you make a sentence with the word?

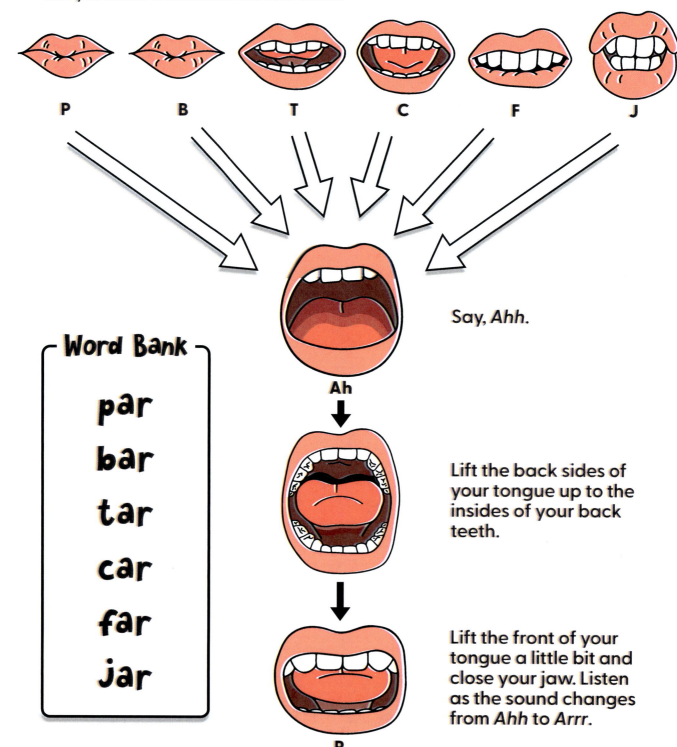

P   B   T   C   F   J

Say, Ahh.

Ah

Lift the back sides of your tongue up to the insides of your back teeth.

Lift the front of your tongue a little bit and close your jaw. Listen as the sound changes from *Ahh* to *Arrr*.

R

Word Bank

par
bar
tar
car
far
jar

Bunched R

Sound-by-Sound® Arrr Practice

Directions: Say each word below. Say it slowly at first, and then say it faster. Mark a box each time you say it. BONUS: Can you make a sentence with the word?

P A R	☐ ☐ ☐ ☐ ☐
B A R	☐ ☐ ☐ ☐ ☐
T A R	☐ ☐ ☐ ☐ ☐
C A R	☐ ☐ ☐ ☐ ☐
F A R	☐ ☐ ☐ ☐ ☐
J A R	☐ ☐ ☐ ☐ ☐

© peachiespeechie.com
Mouths and other visuals may not be transmitted, copied, duplicated or reproduced in whole or part by any means.

Talk Like a Pirate: Say Arrr in Words!

Practice saying your best *Arrr* sound as you say the words below. Say each word three times, and then color in the coin.

Searching for Arrr words

Directions: Name the pictures below and if they have the *Arrr* sound, color them. If they do not have the R sound, do not color them.

Talk like a Pirate and Draw like a Pirate

Directions: Pirates need to be good at drawing so they can draw treasure maps. Practice saying each word below, using your best pirate *Arrr* sound. Then, draw a picture of the word in the space provided.

HEART	STAR	JAR

GARBAGE	CART	YARD

CARD	FARM	GUITAR

Arrr you ready to unscramble the words?

The words below are scrambled. Put the letters in order to make an *Arrr* word. Use the word bank below to help you.

CATR _____

TREHA _____

ASTR _____

ACRDS _____

HCRMA _____

Word Bank

HEART   CARDS   STAR   ALARM   CART   MARCH

Arrr you ready for a word search?

Read the words in the word bank aloud. Practice saying your best *Arrr* sound. Then, search for the words and circle them. Can you find all twelve words, matey?

```
F A C L S P L A R T E S
A R M K P G A V E S B C
R E C H A M C A R T O N
T O N G R O A H I A P L
R C T W K O N F J R K Q
S H V U L N F A X B D C
M A R K E T Y R A S Y T
Z R A E H F J M G C A R
I T K B A I L O M I R N
C A N D Y B A R D L D O
I C H R A R K U M A D E
R T S O L M A R B L E P
```

Word Bank

ARM	MARKET	SPARKLE	FARM
ART	CANDY BAR	CARTON	CAR
CHART	MARBLE	STAR	YARD

Word Search Answer Key

These are the answers to the word search. Were you able to find them all?

```
F A C L   S P L A R T E S
 A R M  K P A G A V E S B C
  R E C H A R C A R T O N
   T O N G R M O A H I A P L
    C T W K O N F J R K Q
   C H V U L N F A X B D C
   M A R K E T Y F R A S Y T
   A  Z A E H F J M G C A R
   R  I T K B A I L O Y I N
   T  C A N D Y B A R D L O
      I C H R A R K U M A D E R
       R T S O L  M A R B L E P
```

Word Bank

ARM	MARKET	SPARKLE	FARM
ART	CANDY BAR	CARTON	CAR
CHART	MARBLE	STAR	YARD

45

Pirate Coarticulation

Directions: As you say the phrases below, your mouth will move into position for the R sound. This is called coarticulation. Start by saying *Arrr* (like the word "are"). Then, blend that word together with the initial R word. It might sound like *ArrrRunning*" for example. Once you can do this, try reading the sentences at the bottom of the page for an additional challenge.

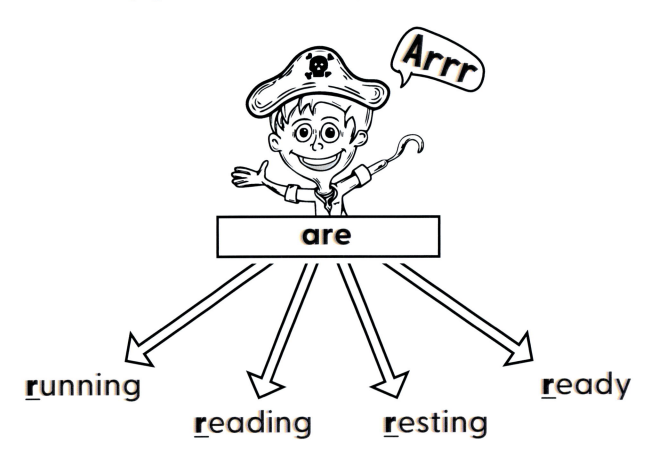

The pirates **are running**.	☐ ☐ ☐ ☐ ☐
The pirates **are reading**.	☐ ☐ ☐ ☐ ☐
The pirates **are resting**.	☐ ☐ ☐ ☐ ☐
The pirates **are ready**.	☐ ☐ ☐ ☐ ☐

© PEACHIESPEECHIE.COM
Mouths and other visuals may not be transmitted, copied, duplicated or reproduced in whole or part by any means.

Talk Like a Pirate: Say Arrr in Phrases!

Say the phrases below. Be sure to use your best pirate *Arrr* sound. Check a dot each time your practice the phrase.

 **Happy st**ar**fish**
◯◯◯◯◯◯◯◯◯◯

 **Sh**ar**k bait**
◯◯◯◯◯◯◯◯◯◯

 **L**ar**ge octopus**
◯◯◯◯◯◯◯◯◯◯

 **F**ar **away**
◯◯◯◯◯◯◯◯◯◯

 **Sh**ar**p cutlass**
◯◯◯◯◯◯◯◯◯◯

 **D**ar**k sea**
◯◯◯◯◯◯◯◯◯◯

© PEACHIESPEECHIE.COM
Mouths and other visuals may not be transmitted, copied, duplicated or reproduced in whole or part by any means.

Arrr you ready to practice?

Say the phrases below. Focus on your tongue placement as you say the word **are**. After practicing, rate your production using the rating scale at the bottom of the page.

Are you ready to go?

We **are** happy.

Are they coming?

They **are** sleepy.

Are you eating lunch?

Self rating: How did I sound?

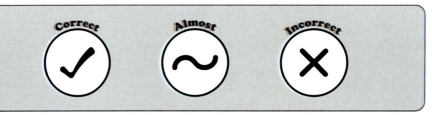

Arrr you ready to practice?

Say the phrases below. Focus on your tongue placement as you say the word **are**. After practicing, rate your production using the rating scale at the bottom of the page.

They **are** running.

Are you calling him?

We **are** thinking about it.

Are the kids laughing?

They **are** waiting for us.

Self rating: How did I sound?

Talk Like a Pirate: Say Arrr in Sentences!

Say the sentences below. Be sure to use your best pirate *Arrr* sound. Check a dot each time you say the sentence.

○○○ The st**ar**fish lives in the deep d**ar**k ocean.

○○○ The pirate has a l**ar**ge, sh**ar**p cutlass.

○○○ The pirates sailed to a f**ar**away island.

○○○ The st**ar**ving octopus ate a candy b**ar**.

○○○ The pirate's dog st**ar**ted b**ar**king.

○○○ They had a p**ar**ty on the pirate ship.

Talk Like a Pirate: Say Arrr in Sentences!

Say the sentences below. Be sure to use your best pirate *Arrr* sound. Check a dot each time you say the sentence.

○○○ The X m**ar**ks the spot on the map.

○○○ He drank pirate juice out of a glass j**ar**.

○○○ The pirate has a tattoo on his **ar**m.

○○○ They had to be sm**ar**t to find the gold.

○○○ Pirates don't drive c**ar**s, they sail ships.

○○○ Captain Stinky f**ar**ted on his ship.

Arrr you ready to practice?

Read the silly sound-loaded sentences below. Focus on your tongue placement when you say the R sound in the bolded words. After practicing, rate your production using the rating scale at the bottom of the page.

The **guard** at the **art** museum played the **harp**.

The magical unicorn bought **stars** and **hearts** at the **market**.

The **farm** animals sneak out at night to dance in the **yard**.

The cats don't **start** playing until after **dark**.

The **artist** made a greeting **card** out of **garbage**.

The **alarm** didn't go off because she **charged** the phone with **marbles**.

Self rating: How did I sound?

Arrr you ready to make sentences?

Directions: Look at the pictures on the left. Say each word aloud, practicing your best *Arrr* sound. Then, make up your own sentence using the word. You can write the sentence on the line, or ask a helper to write the sentence for you.

R Sound Chaining: Pirate Style

Ahoy there! Start by saying the first word in the chain several times. Then, move to the next utterance in the chain. Keep going until you reach the sentence level.

BONUS: Can you make up your own sentences using the bolded phrases below?

Arrr → Bar → Barking → **Dog barking** → There's a dog barking at the pirate.

Arrr → Star → Starting → **Is starting** → The pirate is starting to sing.

Arrr → Par → Party → **Big party** → The pirates are having a big party.

Arrr → Spar → Sparkle → **Coins sparkle** → The coins sparkle in the treasure chest.

Arrr → Arm → Army → **Strong army** → The pirates have a strong army.

Arrr you ready for a Pirate Story?

Read the story below. Focus on production of the **bolded Arrr words** as you read.

Adventure to Starfish Island

On a **dark** and stormy night, Captain **Bart** and his crew set sail. They wanted to find treasure. Captain **Bart** pulled out his map and showed it to the other pirates. "See here, mateys!" he said, "The X **marks** the spot. That's where the gold be, lads!"

The pirates looked at each other and **started** shaking their heads. Pirate **Charlie** spoke up, "Cap'n **Bart**, we all know those **are shark** infested waters. **Are** you sure we should sail that way?" Captain **Bart** nodded and pointed his **sharp** sword into the sky. "I know it be **dark** and dangerous, mateys. There **are sharks** in these **parts**, and maybe ghosts too. But we must keep going to find the treasure."

The pirates were scared, but they sailed on. One pirate played the **guitar** to keep everyone in good spirits. Others played a game of **cards** to pass the time. After many hours, they saw an island in the distance. "**Arrr**! Land ahead!" shouted Captain **Bart**. The pirates all jumped up and **marched** to the side of the ship. "There it is! It's **Starfish** Island, mates!" **Charlie** said. They tossed down the anchor and stopped the ship.

As they walked along the beach, they realized why it was called **Starfish** Island. There were **starfish** everywhere! They kept walking until they found the special place **marked** by an X on the map. The pirates **started** digging. In no time, they found a **large** chest buried in the sand. Together, they pried it open. It was full of gold coins, jewels, and **charm** bracelets. "**Arrr**! We be rich, me **hearties**! Time to celebrate!" cheered Captain **Bart**.

Back on the ship, they had a **party** to celebrate their success. They cheered and danced all night long. They couldn't wait to go on another adventure.

Arrr you ready to answer questions about the story?

After reading the story, Adventure to Starfish Island, answer the questions below.

Who was the captain of the pirate ship?

- Captain Bart
- Pirate Charlie
- Mr. Starfish

What made the dark waters dangerous?

- There were fishermen
- There were sharks
- There were other pirates

Where did the pirates go?

- To Pirate City
- To Never Never Land
- To Starfish Island

What was in the treasure chest?

- Starfish, crabs, and sand
- Coins, jewels, and charm bracelets
- Swords, hats, and hooks

What did the pirates do to celebrate their success?

- They had a party
- They played the guitar
- They gave away the gold

Pirate Hat Instructions

Arrr you ready to make a pirate hat?

Directions:
- Cut out the hat and bottom band and additional hat bands on the following pages.
- Color your hat with markers or crayons.
- Glue the additional hat bands to the bottom band on the hat and wrap around your head to measure how long your band needs to be.
- Trim the ends of the band if desired, and secure the bands with glue or tape.

You can wear your hat while you practice the *Arrr* sound. Best of luck, matey!

Pirate Hat Headband Craft

Cut along the dotted lines. Connect additional strips as needed.

Shark Bite Card Game

Directions: Cut out the cards, shuffle them, and stack them face-down on the table. Take turns drawing cards. If you draw a pirate card, practice saying your best *Arrr* sound. If you draw a shark card, yell, "Shark Bite!" and put all of your cards at the bottom of the stack, including the shark card. Shuffle the cards again, if desired, and keep playing. The first player to collect 5 pirate cards wins. Tip: To make the game easier, put fewer shark cards into the stack.

Shark Bite Card Game

Shark Bite Card Game

Shark Bite Card Game

Talk Like a Pirate: Say Arrr!

Peachie Speechie's Giant Mouth Visuals for the R Sound

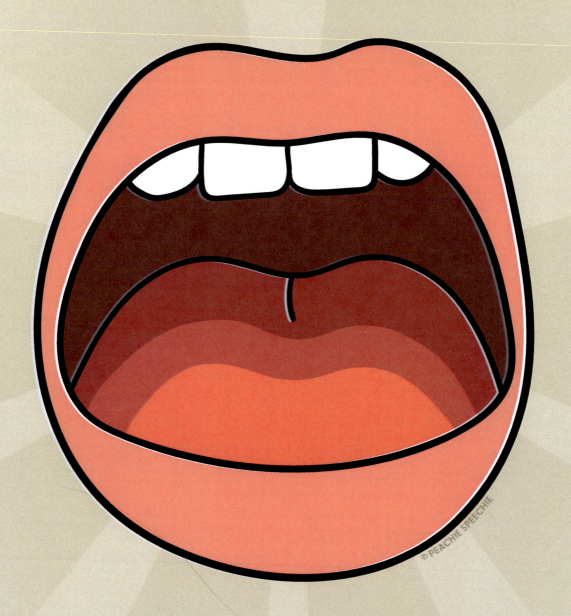

Open your mouth. Say, *Ahh*.

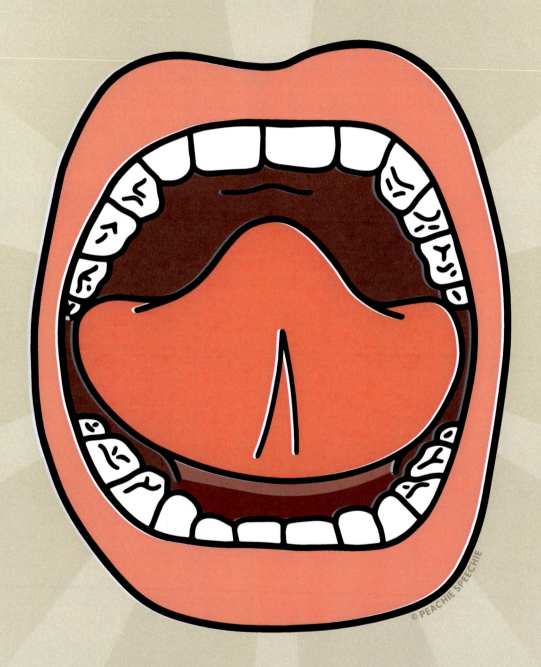

Talk Like a Pirate: Say Arrr!

Peachie Speechie's Giant Mouth Visuals for the R Sound

Retroflex R
Step 3 of 3

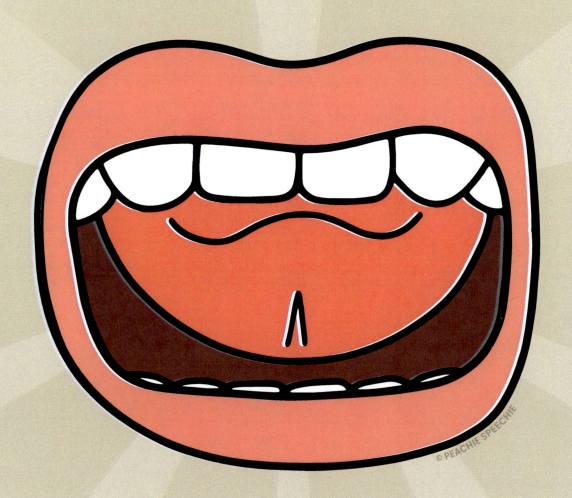

Close your jaw a little bit. Listen as the sound changes from *Ahh* to *Arrr*.

Talk Like a Pirate: Say Arrr!

Peachie Speechie's Giant Mouth Visuals for the R Sound

Bunched R
Step 1 of 3

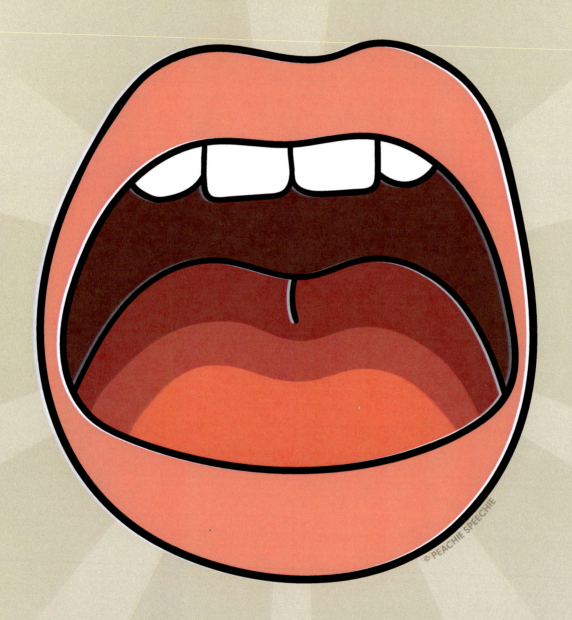

Open your mouth. Say, *Ahh*.

Talk Like a Pirate: Say Arrr!

Peachie Speechie's Giant Mouth Visuals for the R Sound

Bunched R
Step 2 of 3

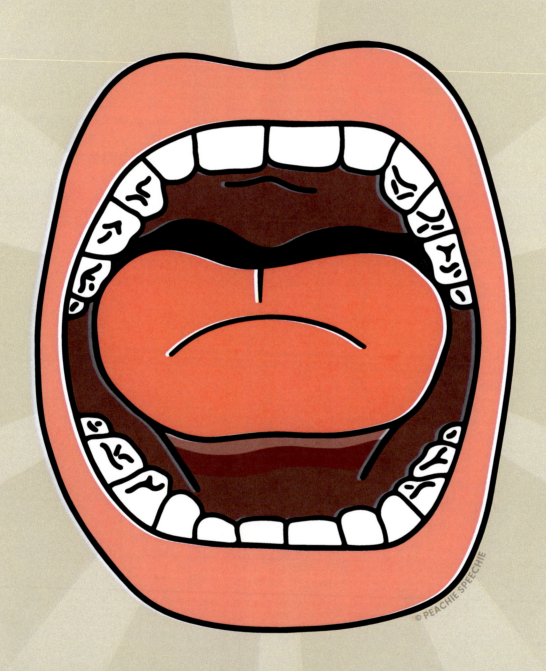

Lift the back sides up to the insides of the back teeth.

Talk Like a Pirate: Say Arrr!

Peachie Speechie's Giant Mouth Visuals for the R Sound

Bunched R
Step 3 of 3

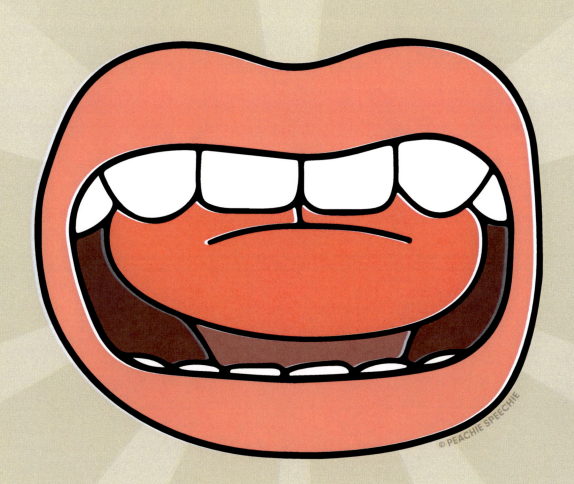

Lift the front of the tongue a little bit and slightly close your jaw. Listen as the sound changes from *Ahh* to *Arrr*.

Peachie Speechie's
Talk Like a Pirate: Say Arrr!

About the Author

Meredith Avren is an ASHA certified speech-language pathologist, public speaker, and author of many popular speech therapy workbooks. She is known for her "I Can Say…" workbook series focusing on remediation of speech sound disorders. She has over 10 years of experience in the school-based setting, and considers the R sound to be her specialty. Meredith graduated from Georgia State University, and lives in the Atlanta area with her graphic designer husband, Josh, and their sons.

Contact Meredith: meredith@peachiespeechie.com

Made in the USA
Las Vegas, NV
16 September 2023

77620412R00050